Barrier-Free Travel

WASHINGTON
NATIONAL PARKS

for Wheelers and Slow Walkers

Candy B. Harrington

PHOTOGRAPHS BY
CHARLES PANNELL

CANDY & CHARLES CREATIVE CONCEPTS

ISBN: 978-0-9985103-2-3

Candy & Charles Creative Concepts
PO Box 278
Ripon, CA 95366-0278

To Charles

Contents

Preface
Second Time's a Charm

Although the cover of this book reflects otherwise, this title could almost be considered a second edition. I say "almost" because the first incarnation only included Olympic and Mount Rainier National Parks, and was titled as such.

It's not that I didn't know about North Cascades National Park back then, it's just that I listened to the nay-sayers who convinced me that the park was totally inaccessible. So I skipped over it on my first go-around. In retrospect that was an enormous error on my part. Granted the North Cascades back country presents some formidable obstacles, even to able-bodied visitors; however upon closer examination I discovered that a portion of the park also boasts several accessible trails, overlooks and scenic drives. And once I discovered this, I just had to go back and correct my previous oversight and make this book a more inclusive resource.

Hence the birth of *Barrier-Free Travel; Washington National Parks for Wheelers and Slow Walkers*.

But that's not the only reason that it was time to update this access guide. There have also been some significant changes to the access in Olympic National Park, especially where the Spruce Creek Railroad Trail is concerned. When completed, this trail will effectively triple the length of accessible trail offerings in the park. Even though the upgrade project still has a way to go, this trail is even more accessible than it was when the "first" edition of this book was published. And although I detailed the progress of the trail so far in this volume, future changes will also be included online, on the book update page at www.barrierfreeolympic.com. So remember to check there before you hit the road.

That said, I have to admit that one of the original reasons for writing the previous edition of this book still stands — to give folks accurate access information about the parks, so they can decide what will and what won't work for them.

I realized a long time ago, that just telling people that something is or isn't accessible is pretty pointless. After all, we all have different abilities, so what's accessible for one person may be insurmountable to another. That's why I've always described the access in all of my books and articles. And that's exactly what I did with everything in this book, including many trails that have simply been described as "accessible with assistance" in other resources.

In the end, this book is about access adequately described — now and in the future — for these three spectacular Washington national parks. And that's something that's sorely needed in the resource department. So go ahead and explore these gems, and let me know how they work for you.

Candy Harrington

candy@EmergingHorizons.com
www.CandyHarrington.com
www.EmergingHorizons.com

Facebook: Candy Harrington
Twitter: Candy B. Harrington
Pinterest: Candy Harrington

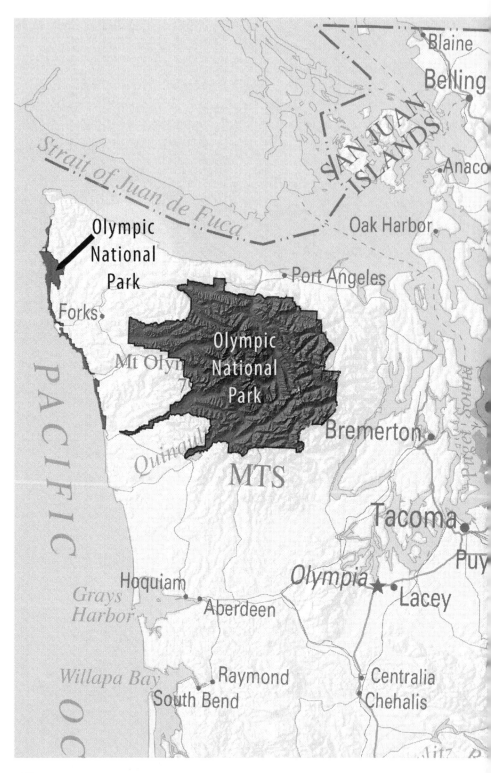

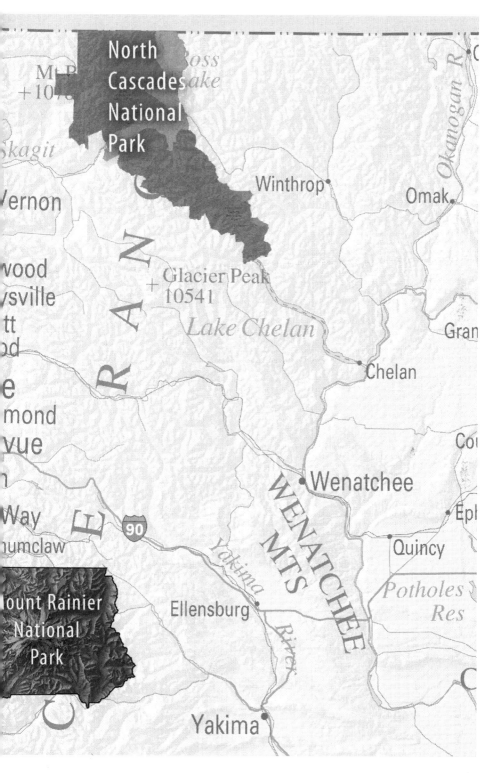

North
Cascades
National
Park

'oss
ake

M R
+10

kagit

/ernon

/ood
/sville
tt
d

e
mond
vue

Way
umclaw

R A N

A

L E

E

Winthrop•

Glacier Peak
10541

Lake Chelan

Chelan

Wenatchee

90

Yakima

WENATCHEE
MTS

River

Ellensburg

ount Rainier
National
Park

Okanogan R.

Omak

Gran

Co

Epl

Quincy

Potholes
Res

Yakima

O

C

Admission, Reservations and Park Passes

Admission Fees

Admission fees to the national parks covered in this book are as follows:

Olympic National Park — $25

Mount Rainier National Park — $25

North Cascades National Park — no admission fee

Fees are collected at park entrance stations, and admission is good for seven days. Payment can be made with cash or a credit card. Save your receipt as you'll need to show it if you enter a park through a different gate, or if you come and go from a park.

At press time, a proposed peak season fee increase for Olympic and Mount Rainier National Parks was under consideration. If adopted, the fees at each of these parks will increase to $70 during the peak seasons. The peak season for Olympic National Park is from May 1 to September 30, and the peak season for Mount Rainier National Park is from June 1 to October 31. Entrance fees will remain unchanged during the rest of the year.

Park Passes

A number of discount park passes are also available at all national park entrance kiosks. See if you qualify for one, as it may help trim your travel budget.

Access Pass

This free lifetime pass provides for free park admission, and is available to U.S. citizens or residents with a permanent disability. Applicants must provide documentation of a permanent disability, and prove residency or citizenship. The pass also offers a 50% discount on campsites and boat launch fees. It generally does not provide for a discount on fees charged by concessionaires.

Military Pass

The free annual Military Pass provides for free park admission, and is available to active members of the Army, Navy, Air Force, Marines and Coast Guard. Reserve and National Guard Members are also eligible. A Common Access Card or Military ID (Form 1173) is required to obtain this pass.

Senior Pass

This lifetime pass provides free park admission, and is available to U.S citizens or permanent residents age 62 or older. The cost of the pass is $80. An annual Senior Pass is also available for $20, and the cost for this annual pass can be applied to the purchase of a lifetime pass. Proof of age and residency or citizenship are required. The pass also offers a 50% discount on campsites and boat launch fees. It generally does not provide for a discount on fees charged by concessionaires.

Annual Pass

If you plan on visiting a number of national parks throughout the year, the Annual Pass may be a good deal for you. This non-transferable pass costs $80 and it's good for free park admission for the entire year. It's an especially attractive deal if you live near a national park, or are planning a road trip that includes a number of national parks. You can also order this pass by calling (888) 275-8747.

Annual 4th Grade Pass

This free annual pass is available to all 4th graders and is valid for the duration of the 4th grade school year and the following summer. Paper vouchers can be obtained at www.everykidinapark.gov and exchanged for an Annual 4th Grade Pass at any national park entrance. This pass is also available to home-schooled students.

Authorized Park Concessionaires

All of the lodgings inside Olympic and Mount Rainier National Parks are operated by authorized concessionaires, who have contracted with the National Park Service, and operate under strict guidelines. They are responsible for the daily operations of the facilities, as well as improvements and upgrades. It's important to deal with these concessionaires directly when you make a reservation; as not only will you get the best prices there, but you will also have access to employees that can block the accessible rooms and describe the access details of each available room. Unfortunately these concessionaires do not always come up first in internet searches because paid advertisements appear before them. Some of these paid advertisements even list "national park lodges" that are located many miles outside the parks, which is very misleading to people who are unfamiliar with the geography of the parks. The authorized concessionaires for the parks covered in this book are listed below. Again, deal directly with these concessionaires for all lodging reservations.

Olympic National Park

Aramark
Lake Crescent Lodge
Sol duc Hot Springs Resort
(888) 896-3818
www.olympicnationalparks.com

Delaware North
Kalaloch Lodge
(866) 662-9928
www.thekalalochlodge.com

Mt. Rainier National Park

Guest Services, Inc.
National Park Inn
Paradise Inn
(855) 755-2275
www.mtrainierguestservices.com

Olympic National Park

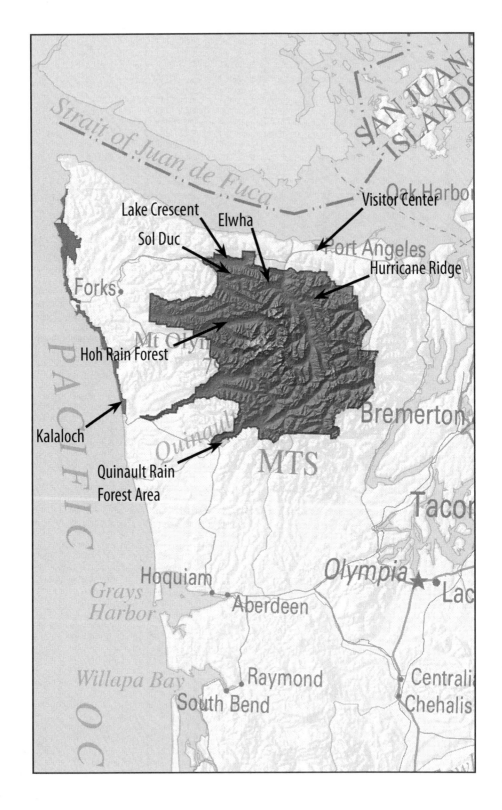

L ocated on Washington's Olympic Peninsula, Olympic National Park occupies nearly one million acres filled with sub-alpine forests, wildflower-filled meadows, rainforest habitat and a rugged coastal shore. The entire park can be accessed from Highway 101, which circumnavigates the Olympic Peninsula; and each area of the park features a small visitor center or ranger station which offers exhibits on the local ecosystem and the history of the area.

The Olympic National Park Visitor Center is located in Port Angeles, which is 80 miles northwest of Seattle. Hurricane Ridge, which offers a great view in a sub-alpine forest, is located south of the main visitor center; while the lowland forests of Lake Crescent and Elwha are located to the west. Sol Duc, which is home to a popular hot springs of the same name, is just a short drive south of Lake Crescent; and the Hoh rainforest is located smack dab in the middle of the park, well off-the-beaten-path. Round it out with Lake Quinault in the south and Kalaloch along the rugged Pacific Coast on the west, and you have a park that's as diverse as it is massive.

The Basics

Road Conditions and Operating Seasons

Although Olympic National Park is open all year, some facilities and roads close in the off season. The Olympic National Park Visitor Center is open year-round, but the regional visitors centers are closed or have reduced days and hours from September to May. Budget cuts and staffing issues can also lead to limited operating hours or seasons, so it's best to check the park website before you make plans.

Road closures are another matter entirely, and with heavy snow the status can change throughout the day in winter months. Highway 101 is open year-round, but some of the park roads may close when weather conditions are bad. Hurricane Ridge Road will close for snow removal, and sometimes when it's actively snowing. Additionally all vehicles are required to carry tire chains when they travel on Hurricane Ridge Road above Heart O' the Hills from November 15 to April 1. Updated road information may be obtained by calling the Road and Weather Hotline at (360) 565-3131.

There will also be temporary delays along Highway 101 near Lake Crescent until 2019. Half-hour delays are expected while the work is in progress to rehabilitate this 12-mile stretch of historic roadway. Traveling outside of work hours — before 8 a.m. and after 6:30 p.m. — can help avoid these delays. No work is performed on weekends or holidays, and work during the summer months can begin two hours after sunrise and must end two hours before sunset. For up-to-the-minute updates on traffic congestion in the area, follow the Olympic National Park twitter feed at twitter.com/OlympicNP.

Altitude

The highest point in Olympic National Park is Mount Olympus with an elevation of 7,980 feet. The rest of the park however, is substantially lower than that, with elevations that range from just above sea level to a little over 5,000 feet. Hurricane Ridge, which is the most easily accessible mountain area in the park, has an elevation of 5,242 feet, and offers panoramic views of the surrounding forest.

Although the symptoms of altitude sickness generally do not appear at elevations under 8,000 feet, wheelchair-users, slow walkers and people with compromised immune systems may feel the effects of increased altitudes at significantly lower elevations. Symptoms can include headaches, dizziness, shortness of breath, lethargy, insomnia and gastrointestinal disturbances. If you are unfamiliar with the effects that higher elevations have on your body, it's best to take it slow and drink plenty of water for the first few days at any increased elevation, especially if you live at sea level. Additionally, you may want to consult your doctor regarding the effects that increased elevations may have on your specific condition. To assist you in your travel planning, the elevations of all the major areas of the park are listed at the beginning of each section.

Airport

The closest commercial airport to Olympic National Park is Seattle-Tacoma International Airport. It's approximately a 3-hour drive from the airport to Port Angeles, and a 2.5-hour drive to Quinault. Accessible van rentals are available from Wheelchair Getaways (800-642-2042), AMS Mobility (800-854-4176) and Mobility Works (877-275-4915) in the Seattle area.

Connectivity

Cell reception in the park is carrier-dependent, and it may be spotty in some areas. Reception is best on Hurricane Ridge and along some sections of Highway 101 near Lake Crescent. You can also get a good signal from campsite 36 in the Sol Duc Campground.

If you have a signal, a free cell phone tour of the park is available by calling (360) 406-5056. It begins with a general overview of the park and then prompts visitors to press the appropriate number for information on a specific area. Locations covered include Hurricane Ridge, Elwha, Lake Crescent, Sol Duc, Mora & Ozette, Hoh, Kalaloch, Quinault and Staircase.

Wheelchair Loans

Manual wheelchairs are available for loan at Hurricane Ridge Visitor Center, Hoh Visitor Center, and Olympic National Park Visitor Center in Port Angeles. They are available on a first-come basis.

Ranger Programs

Free ranger programs, ranger-led walks and evening campground programs are held throughout the park during the summer months. Some of these programs are wheelchair-accessible, depending on their location. Accessibility details of the campground amphitheaters, visitor centers and trails — where these programs are held — are contained in this guide. Consult the park newspaper for the dates and locations of the ranger programs.

Camping

For the most part, campsites in Olympic National Park area available on a first-come basis. The exceptions are at Kalaloch Campground (in the summer) and Sol Duc Campground. Campsites at these campgrounds may be reserved by visiting www.recreation.gov, or by calling (877) 444-6777.

Reservations for accessible sites may require proof of disability upon arrival. If nobody in the party has a need for an accessible site, able-bodied campers may be asked to move to a non-accessible site if a qualified person with a disability has a need for the accessible site. Accessible sites may not be reserved by able-bodied campers unless they are the only sites left at the time of reservation.

Port Angeles *Elevation 56 Feet*

L ocated about three hours northwest of Seattle, Port Angeles is home to the main visitor center for the park. It's also the best place to get gas, stock up on supplies, do laundry and grab a bite to eat.

Olympic National Park Visitor Center
3002 Mt. Angeles Road
Port Angeles, WA 98362
(360) 565-3130

The Olympic National Park Visitor Center features accessible parking with ramp access up to the front entrance. Inside there are interpretive exhibits that present a good overview of the park, and a ranger on duty to answer questions. Accessible restrooms are also located inside.

Out back you'll find the .4-mile Living Forest Trail. This loop trail, which is rated as "accessible with assistance", leads through the forest and features a nice view of Peabody Creek Valley. The hard-packed dirt trail is covered in crushed granite, but it's almost asphalt-like in some places due to heavy use. There is a little duff over other parts of the trail, and at one point the trail narrows to 30-inches wide. That narrowing is due to the overgrowth of brush, and it varies depending on the time of year.

One bridge has a 1.5-inch lip, and most manual wheelchair-users will need assistance on one steep switchback for a few feet. Other than that,

The Olympic National Park Visitor Center

The Living Forest Trail

it's fairly level and smooth, and it makes for easy rolling. There's also an accessible picnic table in a shady grove near the parking lot, which makes a good lunch time stop.

Lake Crescent

L ocated 18 miles west of Port Angeles, Lake Crescent is one of the crown jewels of Olympic National Park. This glacially formed lake is 624-feet deep, and it's filled with crystal clear blue-green water. And because of the lack of nitrogen, there's very little plant life below the surface. The end result is a pristine mountain lake, which offers accessible trails, picnic areas and attractions on both shores.

Attractions

Storm King Ranger Station

Storm King Ranger Station is located at the east end of Lake Crescent Road, near Lake Crescent Lodge. There's accessible parking in the adjacent lot, with ramped access to the building. Inside, there's plenty of room to maneuver a wheelchair through the book store and over to the information desk. Accessible flush toilets and shaded accessible picnic tables are located next to the building. The Storm king Ranger Station is open intermittently during the summer, and closed the rest of the year.

Moments in Time Nature Trail

Marymere Falls Trail

Trails

Moments in Time Nature Trail

The Moments in Time Nature Trail can be easily accessed from Lake Crescent Lodge. Just head east on the paved trail along the lakeshore until you hit the .8-mile loop trail. This hard-packed dirt trail is covered with crushed granite, and outside of a few roots here and there, it's nicely accessible. And as far as the roots and ruts go — they are there, but they're easy to dodge. This easy trail winds through the mature forest and around some old homestead sites; and although it's rated as "accessible with assistance", it's doable for most wheelchair-users and slow walkers.

Marymere Falls Trail

The Marymere Falls Trail — which is rated as "accessible with assistance" for the first half-mile — begins behind the Storm King Ranger Station. The hard-packed dirt trail splits in two a short way from the trailhead, and the left fork goes down to the beach. Although the beach spur is only 30 feet long, it's too steep for most wheelchair-users and slow walkers. The main trail is fairly level until it reaches the freeway underpass, but after that it has a sustained 1:7 grade, with no level spots to rest. Once the trail passes the Mt. Storm King Trail the grade increases; but it's still doable for some power wheelchair- and scooter-uses until it crosses Barnes Creek. After that, there's a stump in the middle of the trail which blocks further access. Although wheelchair-users and slow walkers won't be able to make it all the way to Marymere Falls, it's still a nice stroll along the creek through an old growth forest. Do as much as you can, then turn back when the grade becomes too difficult.

Spruce Railroad Trail

Currently the Spruce Railroad Trail is in a state of transition. Located on the north shore of Lake Crescent, the trail follows the historic grade of the Spruce Railroad, which was abandoned in 1951. At this time the trail is divided into an east section and a west section, which are separated by the recently refurbished McFee Tunnel.

The trailhead for the west section of the Spruce Railroad Trail is located along Camp David Jr. Road, which is just west of the Fairholme General Store, along Highway 101. The first part of this road is paved, but after the 1.5-mile point it turns into a graded dirt road. Although the latter section of the road is a bit bumpy, it's still passable in a low clearance vehicle in dry weather. The trailhead for the Spruce Railroad

The Spruce Railroad Trail

Trail is located at about the three-mile point on the left side of the road. It's marked by a single accessible parking space and three standard parking spaces on the right side of the road. There are no facilities at the trailhead.

The path on the left leads up to the trailhead — go right at the trailhead to stay in the park and travel along Lake Crescent. This paved multi-use trail passes through a spruce, fir and alder forest, however it loses its access at the two mile point, just after milepost 29. Plans are underway to pave the remaining eight miles of the trail to the east. The Spruce Railroad Trail will eventually connect with the 130-mile Olympic Discovery Trail on the east and west sides of the park.

The trailhead for the east section of the Spruce Railroad Trail (Lyre Creek Trailhead) is located off of East Beach Road on the way to Log Cabin Resort. Follow the road for about three miles from Highway 101, then turn left on Boundary Creek Road and follow the signs to the trailhead. There is an accessible vault toilet in the parking lot, and level access over to the trailhead. A new larger parking lot is set to be constructed at this trailhead. This part of the trail is accessible for about a third-mile, before it reverts back to the inaccessible incarnation.

At this time the entire length of the Spruce Railroad Trail is expected to be paved and fully wheelchair-accessible by the end of 2019.

Picnic Areas

Bovee's Meadows Picnic Area

Located west of Lake Crescent Lodge on Lake Crescent Road, Bovee's Meadow Picnic Area has some usable spots on the lakeshore, with accessible vault toilets located nearby.

La Poel Picnic Area

La Poel Picnic Area is located on the south shore of Lake Crescent off Highway 101, west of Lake Crescent Lodge. It's accessed by a low clearance bumpy road through the forest, that's not suitable for RVs. Several picnic tables offer good access and a level surface; and although the accessible vault toilet has grab bars, there is a four-inch step up to it because of erosion.

East Beach Picnic Area

East Beach Picnic Area is located on the north shore of Lake Crescent, off East Beach Road near the Highway 101 junction. There are several picnic tables located on a level surface near the dirt parking area. An accessible vault toilet is located nearby. Although the road is fairly steep, the picnic area offers a nice lake view.

North Shore Picnic Area

Located along the north shore of Lake Crescent, this picnic area is relatively secluded. It includes accessible picnic tables and an accessible vault toilet. And although it requires a drive down a graded dirt road, it's still quite doable in a low clearance vehicle in dry weather.

Lodging

Lake Crescent Lodge

416 Lake Crescent Road
Port Angeles, WA 98363
(888) 896-3618
www.olympicnationalparks.com

Lake Crescent Lodge

Room 101 in the Marymere wing at Lake Crescent Lodge

Built in 1915, Lake Crescent Lodge is the oldest property in Olympic National Park. That said, access upgrades have been added over the years, with the newest addition being the accessible Marymere wing.

There is accessible parking near the main lodge with barrier-free access to the front lobby. From there it's just a short roll on a paved sidewalk to the lakeside Marymere building.

Room 101 features wide doorways and good pathway access. It's furnished with two 24-inch high queen-sized beds, with wheelchair

Bathroom in room 101 in the Marymere wing at Lake Crescent Lodge

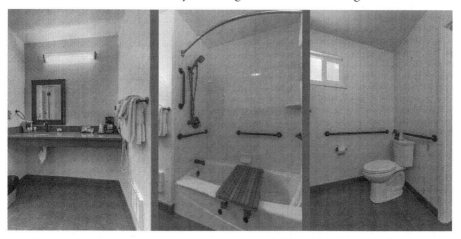

Room 300 in the Pyramid Mountain Building at Lake Crescent Lodge

access on both sides. The bathroom features a full five-foot turning radius, and it's equipped with a tub/shower combination with grab bars, a hand-held showerhead and a wooden shower bench. The toilet grab bars are located on the back and right walls (as seated), and the bathroom also includes a roll-under sink. A plastic shower chair is available upon request.

There is a slight 3/4-inch lip at the back door, which leads out to a shared

Bathroom in room 300 in the Pyramid Mountain Building at Lake Crescent Lodge

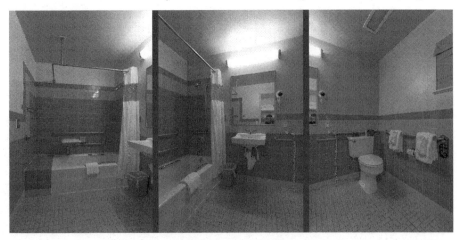

porch that's furnished with two chairs. Although there's plenty of room to maneuver a wheelchair, you can always move the chairs if the space is too tight.

Room 102, which is located next door, has the same access features.

The Pyramid Mountain rooms, which are located across the parking lot, offer a forest setting and a nice meadow view. Room 300 in the Pyramid Building is not flagged as an accessible room, but it may work for some slow walkers.

There's accessible parking near the room with level access over to the front door. The room features wide doorways, good pathway access, a lowered peephole and a lowered clothing rod. It's furnished with a 25-inch high queen-sized platform bed with wheelchair access on both sides, two large easy chairs, a small table and two bedside tables. There's also level access out the back door to a small semi-private patio; however one of the easy chairs may have to be moved for optimal pathway access.

The bathroom has a full five-foot turning radius and is equipped with a tub/shower combination with grab bars. There is no hand-held showerhead; and although there is a fold-down shower bench installed at the far end of the tub, it appears to be installed incorrectly, as the bottom is a full 10-12 inches from the top of the tub. It's basically unusable, but it can be folded up out of the way. A plastic shower chair is also available. Other

Sunset on Lake Crescent

bathroom access features include a toilet with grab bars on the left and back walls (as seated), and a roll-under sink with a lowered mirror.

This corner room is a bit farther from the lake than the Marymere rooms, but it still has a partial lake view. It's certainly spacious enough to accommodate a wheelchair or even a large scooter, if you can make the bathroom work for you. Additionally since it's not listed in the accessible room inventory, you'll have to specifically request room 300 when you make a reservation.

The Singer Tavern Cottages may also work for some slow walkers. They don't have any access features, but they are located close to the main lodge.

All of the public areas in the main lodge building are accessible. This former tavern once housed sleeping rooms upstairs, and although there are still lodge rooms on the second floor, there is no elevator.

Lake Crescent Lodge is open from late April to early January.

Fairholme Campground

Fairholme Campground is located on the west side of Lake Crescent on Camp David Jr. Road, near the Fairholme General Store. Campsite A16 has paved parking, an accessible picnic table and grill, and a level tent pad. It's located across from the restrooms, which have level access and are equipped with accessible stalls and roll-under sinks. This campground is open from May to October, and campsites are available on a walk-in basis.

Dining

Lake Crescent Lodge Dining Room

The Lake Crescent Lodge Dining Room is located just off the hotel lobby. It features level access with plenty of room to navigate a wheelchair. This lakeside restaurant serves breakfast, lunch and dinner, and features creative Pacific Northwest fare. The dining room also offers a nice selection of local wines, and features a good view of the lake. Dinner reservations are highly recommended, especially on the weekends.

Lake Crescent Lodge Lounge

Located on a portion of the glassed-in porch, just off the hotel lobby, the Lake Crescent Lodge Lounge features level access and ample wheelchair clearance around the tables. It offers a nice view of the lake, and the menu includes a good sampling of casual fare, from appetizers and sandwiches, to soups, salads and light entrees. It's also the perfect place to watch the sunset over the lake and enjoy a glass of wine or a drink from the bar.

Sunnyside Cafe

Sunnyside Cafe is located in Log Cabin Resort on the north shore of Lake Crescent. Just take East Beach Road off of Highway 101, and follow the road until you come to the lodge on your left. There is accessible parking in front of the lodge, with level access to the main lobby and the Sunnyside Cafe. A hot buffet breakfast is served up every morning, while sandwiches, salads, pasta dishes and entrees are available the rest of the day. The cafe offers a great view of the lake, and outside accessible seating is also available. Log Cabin Resort is open from May to September.

Services

Fairholme General Store

Located on the north side of Highway 101 near Camp David Jr. Road, the Fairholme General Store offers a nice selection of sandwiches, snacks and ice cream, as well as camping supplies, souvenirs and groceries. There's accessible parking near the ramp up to the front door, and level access to the standard picnic tables in a nearby grassy area. Although the picnic tables aren't accessible models, there may be room enough at the ends for some wheelchair-users. The store is open from Memorial Day to Labor Day.

Sol Duc
.... *Elevation 2,000 Feet*

The Sol Duc area is located south of Lake Crescent along the Sol Duc River. The landscape is comprised of an old growth forest, sub-alpine lakes, and a river which serves as a highway for Coho salmon on their yearly migration. It's also the site of thermal waters that are piped into the resort's pools for park guests to enjoy.

Attractions

Sol Duc Hot Springs

There's ramp access to the Sol Duc Hot Springs front office, with barrier-free access to the pools in back. The pool area features good pathway access, and the complex also includes barrier-free changing rooms and accessible restrooms. The mineral wading pool is reserved for children under three, but the Large Mineral Fountain Pool (101°) and the Freshwater Pool (50° - 80°, depending on the season) feature ramp access. There is also a portable pool lift available for these pools or for the Medium Mineral Pool (104°), which isn't ramped. Admission to the pools is free for Sol Duc Hot Springs Resort guests,

The Large Mineral Fountain Pool at Sol Duc Hot Springs Resort

but others can purchase a day-use pass. A loaner wheelchair is available on a first-come basis.

Trails

Salmon Cascades

Located along Sol Duc Road, Salmon Cascades is a good place to catch a glimpse of the migrating salmon. There is accessible parking near a picnic table on a level gravel area. An accessible vault toilet is located nearby, and although it has grab bars, there is a two-inch step up to it because of erosion. A hard-packed dirt trail leads from the accessible parking area out to the Salmon Cascades overlook. The trail is wide and level and doable for most folks. The best time to spot the salmon leaping over the falls is in late October and early November, but it's still a scenic stop the rest of the year.

Trail to the Salmon Cascades overlook

Lodging

Sol Duc Hot Springs Resort

12076 Sol Duc Hot Springs Road
Port Angeles, WA 98363
(888) 896-3618
www.olympicnationalparks.com

Sol Duc Hot Springs Resort shares an office with Sol Duc Hot Springs. Cabin 132 is located just a short drive away, with accessible parking available in back. There is ramp access from the parking area up to the cabin, which features a wide doorway and good pathway access. It's furnished with two 28-inch high double beds with an access aisle between them, an easy chair and a dining table with two chairs. The bathroom is equipped with a tub/shower combination with grab bars. There is also a roll-under sink in the bathroom, but the toilet lacks grab bars. A portable shower chair is available upon request.

There is level access to a large grassy area in front of the cabin, which features a picnic table. There is also plenty of room to roll around on the front porch, which is furnished with a small bench.

Cabins 133 and 132 share a ramp between them at the Sol Duc Hot Springs Resort

Inside Cabin 132 at the Sol Duc Hot Springs Resort

Cabin 133 and Cabin 111 have the same access features as Cabin 132, but Cabin 111 also has a small kitchen.

The resort is open from March to October.

Bathroom in Cabin 132 at the Sol Duc Hot Springs Resort

Sol Duc Campground

The Sol Duc Campground is located down the road from the Sol Duc Hot Springs Resort. Campsite 36 includes accessible parking, an accessible picnic table and grill, and a level tent pad. It's located across from the accessible restrooms, which are equipped with accessible stalls and roll-under sinks. There is a path to the amphitheater from the campground, but wheelchair-users will most likely require assistance up the last hill. Wheelchair seating is available in front. There is also an amphitheater parking lot along Sol Duc Hot Springs Road, however it lacks accessible spaces, and the path to the campground is not wheelchair-accessible. Reservations for the Sol Duc Campground can be made at www. recreation.gov or (877) 444-6777, from 3 days to 12 months in advance. The campground is fully open from March through October, but primitive camping is available in the winter when Sol Duc Road is open.

Sol Duc Resort RV Park

The Sol Duc Resort RV Park is located along Sol Duc Hot Springs Road between the Sol Duc Hot Springs Resort and the Sol Duc Campground. Sites 16 and 17 are wheelchair-accessible, and have level access and accessible picnic tables and fire rings. The sites also have water and power. A dump station is available for an additional fee. Reservations for the Sol Duc Resort RV Park can be made at www.recreation.gov or (877) 444-6777. The RV park is open from March through October.

Dining

Springs Restaurant

There's level access to the Springs Restaurant, which is located near the Sol Duc Hot Springs Resort office. The restaurant is open for breakfast, lunch and dinner. Breakfast offerings include a large selection of standard favorites, while the lunch menu features a variety of soups, salads and sandwiches. Dinner is a real treat at the Springs Restaurant, as the chefs prepare an impressive selection of Northwestern favorites made from locally sourced ingredients.

Elwha *Elevation 3,655 Feet*

The Elwha Valley is located southeast of Lake Crescent, along Olympic Hot Springs Road, off of Highway 101. Not only is this area the site of one of the largest ecosystem restoration projects in National Park Service History; but it also offers some of the best scenery in the park, with the sparkling Elwha River framed by the majestic Olympic Mountains.

Attractions

Elwha Ranger Station

The historic Elwha Ranger Station was built in the 1930s, but access upgrades were added to the building in 2015. Today it sports ramp access, accessible restrooms and accessible parking out in front. The ranger station offers general park information and is open intermittently during the summer months. Standard picnic tables are located in the turnout next to the ranger station, and although they are not technically accessible they may be usable for some folks. There are no striped spaces in the turnout, but there's plenty of room to park parallel and deploy a lift or ramp.

Glines Canyon Spillway Overlook

The Glines Canyon Spillway Overlook offers an interesting perspective on the result of the Elwha Dam Restoration Project. This massive undertaking began in September 2011 with the removal of the Elwha and Glines Canyon Dams on the Elwha River. Now that both dams are gone and Lake Mills and Lake Aldwell reservoirs have been drained, the Elwha River flows freely through the Olympic Mountains to the Pacific Ocean. As a result, salmon and trout are once again migrating past the former dam sites for the first time in over 100 years.

There's accessible parking with level access to the Glines Canyon Spillway Overlook, which leads out over the top of the former spillway. Interpretive panels and audio kiosks dot the short path to the overlook, but the big attraction of this site is the view down into the river. It should be noted that this was the largest dam ever to be removed in the United States. There is also an accessible vault toilet near the parking area.

Glines Canyon

Trails

Madison Falls

One of the most accessible waterfalls in the park — Madison Falls —
is located on Olympic Hot Springs Road, just south of Highway 101.
There's accessible parking next to a large grassy picnic area which has
accessible picnic tables. Accessible vault toilets are located nearby. A
.1-mile paved level trail leads from the picnic area through the forest to the
base of Madison Falls. The overlook features lowered railings for optimal
wheelchair viewing, as well as a bench for slow walkers. From the main
parking area you can also get a good view of the Elwha River across the
street. Additionally, there's a level hard-packed dirt viewing area on the
other side of the road, if you'd like to get a closer look of the river.

Lodging

Campground Closures

There are currently no campgrounds in the Elwha Valley. They were closed
after they were damaged in the 2016 floods.

Hurricane Ridge

Elevation 5,242 Feet

Hurricane Ridge, which is located south of Olympic National Park Visitor Center on Hurricane Ridge Road, features sweeping views of sub-alpine forests and wildflower-filled meadows. It's aptly named, as it's not uncommon for the wind to gust up to 75 miles-per-hour on the ridge top. And with 30 to 35 feet of snow every year, this area is continually being reshaped by the elements.

Attractions

Hurricane Ridge Visitor Center

The Hurricane Ridge Visitor Center features accessible parking near the entrance, and level access to the building. Since the visitor center is built into the side of the mountain, the main entrance is on the second floor. There's barrier-free access throughout the building, with level access to the theater and around the interpretive exhibits. Although there is a good view from second floor, wheelchair-users can't see much because of the high windows. There's a better view out on the second-floor deck, but for the best unobstructed view, head down to the first floor. There's only stairway

The view from Hurricane Ridge

access from the second floor, but there's ramp access to the lower viewing area from the parking lot. A wheelchair-height viewing scope is located on the lower deck, and there's plenty of room to navigate a wheelchair around this 5,242-foot high vantage point. Accessible restrooms are also located on the lower level.

Trails

Meadow Trails

The Cirque Rim Trail and the Big Meadow Loop, which are located near the visitor center, are rated as "accessible with assistance". These trails are paved, but the first 100-foot stretch that leads out to the rim overlook has a 1:8 or greater grade. This part would be difficult if not impossible for most manual wheelchair-users, however it may be doable for folks with scooters or power wheelchairs. If you can make it past the first 100 feet, turn right at the overlook and follow the Cirque Rim Trail for a half-mile, then loop back on the Big Meadow Loop segment for another quarter-mile. The trails are fairly level and they offer sweeping views of Port Angeles, the Juan de Fuca Strait and the Olympic Mountains.

Lodging

Heart O' the Hills Campground

Heart O' the Hills Campground is located on Hurricane Ridge Road, halfway between the Olympic National Park Visitor Center and the Hurricane Ridge Visitor Center. Campsite A19 is paved and features accessible parking, an accessible table and grill, and a level tent site. It's located across the street from the restroom which has accessible stalls and roll-under sinks. The path to the amphitheater is located just past Loop B, but it's too steep and not wheelchair-accessible. This campground is open year-round, and campsites are available on a walk-in basis.

Hoh Rain Forest

Named for the Native Americans that originally inhabited the area, Hoh Rain Forest is located south of Sol Duc, along the Hoh River. It gets a whopping 12 feet of precipitation per year and it's home to massive conifers that dominate the landscape. Add in a healthy sprinkling of mosses and ferns that cover the forest floor, and decaying trees that serve as nurse logs, and the result is the perfect example of a temperate rainforest.

Attractions

Hoh Rain Forest Visitor Center

There's accessible parking near the Hoh Rain Forest Visitor Center, with level access to the front door. The building, which was remodeled in 2014, features interpretive exhibits about the rainforest and a ranger-staffed information desk. Accessible restrooms are also located in the visitor center.

Hall of Mosses Trail in the Hoh Rain Forest

Trails

Mini Rain Forest Trail

The Mini Rain Forest Trail, which is rated as "accessible with assistance", begins on the back porch of the visitor center. This quarter-mile flat paved trail winds through the old growth forest before it loops back to the parking lot.

Hall of Mosses Trail

The trailhead to the Hall of Mosses Trail is located at the .1 mile point along the Mini Rain Forest Trail. This hard-packed trail is level and doable for about 75 yards. Once you hit the bridge it loses its access, as the grade gets steeper and there are steps along the way. Still it's a nice stroll through the rainforest, and you can see salmon in river below during the fall. Combined with the Mini Rain Forest Trail, it makes a short accessible hike.

Picnic Areas

Hoh Picnic Area

The Hoh Picnic Area features accessible parking with curb-cut access over to a paved path through the picnic area. Accessible picnic tables are available in a level shaded area, and an accessible restroom is located on the far side of the picnic area. This is a favorite picnic area for groups, so it's pretty crowded in peak season. Alternatively there are shaded pullouts along Upper Hoh Road, and although they lack picnic tables, they may make do in a pinch for a makeshift picnic.

Lodging

Hoh Campground

Hoh Campground is located near the visitor center, next to the Hoh Picnic Area. It includes accessible campsites, picnic tables and restrooms in Loop A. The amphitheater is also accessible. This campground is open year-round, and campsites are available on a walk-in basis.

Kalaloch

Elevation 31 Feet

Located on a coastal strip of the national park, Kalaloch means "a good place to land" in the Quinault language. And with rugged coastal views, quiet beaches, and fog-shrouded inlets, the name seems fitting.

Attractions

Beach Four

Beach Four is located north of Kalaloch Lodge, off of Highway 101. There's accessible parking near the accessible vault toilets, and level access over to the trailhead. The hard-packed dirt trail on the right has some large rocks near the beginning, but they are pretty easy to dodge. Still, some folks may need a little assistance. The level trail leads out to a beach overlook, which has plenty of room for a wheelchair. There is also a bench there for slow walkers, and it's a pleasant spot to enjoy the ocean. The other trail (the one on the left) goes down to the beach, but it's very steep and not accessible. There is also a picnic table on a level grassy area near the parking lot. It's pretty high (most likely from erosion), but you can always improvise and use the bench for a table.

Beach Four near Kalaloch

Ruby Beach

Ruby Beach is located north of Beach Four, off of Highway 101. A graded dirt road leads down to a level dirt parking area near the accessible restrooms, but the small lot is not striped. There is a short dirt path out to the beach overlook. Depending on the condition of the trail, some wheelchair-users may need assistance dodging the few rocks and bumps along the way. The overlook sits above a log strewn beach and offers some nice ocean views. There is also an accessible picnic table at the top of the drive, near the beginning of the dirt road. There is level access to the picnic table, but wheelchair-users might need a little assistance getting all the way out to the adjacent viewpoint.

Lodging

Kalaloch Lodge

157151 US 101
Forks, WA 98331
(866) 662-9928
www.thekalalochlodge.com

This rustic but comfortable lodge offers two accessible cabins, with great coastal views. Accessible parking is available in front of the main building, and there is ramp access up to the restaurant in front. There are steps down into the adjacent gift shop, which also doubles as the office; however, there is level access to the gift shop via a sliding glass door in the back. Just head to the left of the building from the accessible parking spot.

Cabin 40, which is located near the office, features reserved parking in a large level area. The parking space isn't striped, but there's plenty of room for an accessible van. There's ramp access up to the front door of this duplex cabin, which features wide doorways and barrier-free pathway access.

The large kitchen has a roll-under counter and it's equipped with a refrigerator, stove, microwave and a coffeemaker. There are plenty of pots, pans, dishes and glasses, and the kitchen also has a roll-under sink. The dining table has four bar chairs, and there is additional bar seating at the kitchen counter. The living room has an 18-inch high double futon, two easy chairs and a wood burning stove. There is also a coffee table in front of the futon, which makes this a good accessible place to enjoy a meal by the fire.

The adjacent bedroom is furnished with two 30-inch high queen-sized beds with an access aisle between them. There is a wide doorway into the bathroom which has a full five-foot turning radius and is equipped with a large roll-in shower (six feet wide, and four feet deep) with grab bars, a hand-held showerhead and a portable shower chair. The toilet has a grab bar on the right side (as seated), and there is also a roll-under sink with a lowered mirror in the bathroom. They even remembered the small touches like lowered robe hooks, and a lowered soap dispenser in the shower.

Outside there's an accessible picnic table on a level grassy spot. And if you'd like to explore the area, the cabin is equipped with some walking sticks and a pair of binoculars.

A gazebo that overlooks the beach is just a short walk away, but there's also an accessible parking space there if you'd prefer to drive. There's a small bump up to the gazebo, but it's manageable with a little assistance. Alternatively there's level access to picnic tables on the adjacent grassy area, which offer equally stunning ocean views.

Cabin 43, which is rated as "partially accessible", is located next to the gazebo area. It has the same access features as Cabin 40, except that it has a tub/shower combination instead of a roll-in shower in the bathroom.

Office, gift shop and restaurant at Kalaloch Lodge

Bedroom in Cabin 40 at Kalaloch Lodge

Bathroom in Cabin 40 at Kalaloch Lodge

Kalaloch Campground

Kalaloch Campground is located north of Kalaloch Lodge, off of Highway 101. Campsites A9, D18 and D30 all include an accessible table and grill, and a level tent site. They are located near restrooms that have accessible stalls and roll-under sinks. There is also a level path to the amphitheater, which has wheelchair seating in front and on the sides. The campground registration parking lot has accessible parking with level access to the registration area, and a barrier-free pathway to some accessible picnic tables on a grassy median. There is also a path to the amphitheater from the campground registration lot, and although it's a bit bumpy, it's still doable for most folks. Kalaloch Campground is open year-round, and campsites are reservable in the summer at www.recreation.gov or (877) 444-6777.

Dining

Creekside Restaurant

There's level access to the Creekside Restaurant from the front lodge entrance, and plenty of room to navigate a wheelchair between the tables. The restaurant is open for breakfast, lunch and dinner; and the menu includes calorie counts on select items. Gluten-free, dairy-free, organic and small portion selections are also available.

Services

Mercantile

There is level access to the Mercantile, which is located across the parking lot from the office. It stocks a good selection of snacks, chips, ice cream, beverages, canned goods and wine. Accessible restrooms are located next door.

Quinault Rain Forest Area *Elevation 200 Feet*

Located in the far south area of the park, Lake Quinault is surrounded by a temperate rainforest. The lake itself falls under the jurisdiction of the Quinault Indian Nation, while the north shore is located inside Olympic National Park, and the south shore is outside the park boundaries.

Attractions

Quinault Rain Forest Ranger Station

The Quinault Rain Forest Ranger Station is located on the north side of the lake on N. Shore Road. Parking is available in a large level dirt area; and although it's not striped, there's plenty of room for an accessible van. The ranger station features level access, and it's open intermittently in the summer, when a ranger is on duty. Accessible restrooms and a picnic table on a level grassy area are located near the parking lot.

Trails

Maple Glade Trail

The trailhead for the Maple Glade Trail is near the parking area at the Quinault Rain Forest Ranger Station. This half-mile hard-packed dirt trail is covered with crushed granite, and is rated as "accessible with assistance". The trail is fairly level, but there are a few bumps here and there, and it narrows to about two-feet wide in a few places. It's a pleasant stroll under the forest canopy, with bridges over the damp areas along the route. You can do this as a loop trail, or connect to the Kestner Homestead Trail along the way.

Kestner Homestead Trail

The trailhead for the Kestner Homestead Trail is near the picnic area at the Quinault Rain Forest Ranger Station. This 1.3-mile hard-packed dirt trail is covered in crushed granite, and is rated as "accessible with assistance". It's fairly level, with barrier-free access over a wooden bridge that leads to the abandoned homestead. There's a level path around the homestead, which is littered with dilapidated farm buildings and vintage equipment. There is also a picnic shelter at the homestead, and although there are no accessible tables there, it does have level access. After the homestead, the trail winds back through the rainforest, passes the Maple Glade Trail, and returns to the trailhead. There are some large pieces of gravel on the two-to-three-foot wide trail, but for the most part they are easy to avoid. Additionally, because of the dirt surface, this trail is best done in dry weather.

Rain Forest Nature Loop

The Rain Forest Nature Loop is located on the south side of the lake, outside of Olympic National Park. Accessible parking is available near the trailhead, with accessible restrooms across the parking lot. There is also a picnic table on a flat level surface near the parking lot. This half-mile loop trail is rated as accessible, but in reality, only the first part is doable for wheelchair-users and slow walkers. Although this part of the hard-packed dirt trail is wide and level, after it reaches Willoughby Creek the grade substantially increases and there are exposed tree roots, ruts and even steps along the way. That said, it's still worth a stop as it's a beautiful walk through the rainforest, and the Willoughby Creek Overlook has lowered rails for optimal wheelchair viewing. Some folks might also be able to do

The Kestner Homestead

the last part of the trail in reverse, but the grade significantly increases after the short accessible section in the beginning.

Lodging

Lake Quinault Lodge

345 S. Shore Road
Quinault, WA 98575
(888) 896-3818
www.olympicnationalparks.com

Located on the south shore of the lake, outside Olympic National Park, Lake Quinault Lodge dates back to 1926. Accessible parking is located in the front with level access to the lobby and gift shop.

Room 402, which is an accessible lake view room, is located in back, with accessible parking nearby. It features wide doorways and good pathway access and it's furnished with a 27-inch high queen-sized bed with wheelchair access on both sides. There is also a 12-inch high double sofa bed in the room.

The bathroom has a full five-foot turning radius and it's equipped with a roll-in shower with grab bars, a hand-held showerhead and a shower chair. The toilet grab bars are located on the right and back walls (as seated), and the bathroom also has a roll-under sink.

Room 403 has the exact same access features.

The Fireplace Rooms might also be doable for some slow walkers. These rooms have wide doorways and good pathway access, but the bathrooms don't have roll-under sinks or toilet grab bars; and instead of roll-in showers they are equipped with low-step showers. A portable shower chair and a toilet riser are available upon request. Each room is furnished with a 27-inch high king-size bed, an easy chair, a refrigerator; and as the name implies, a fireplace. There is a five-inch step out to the patio, which borders on a grassy area. There are eight fireplace rooms on the first floor and eight on the second floor. There is no elevator in the building, but because it's built on a slope, the second floor can be accessed from the front lobby if you can manage three steps. Although these premium rooms are not technically accessible, they may work for some slow walkers.

Lake Quinault Lodge

Room 402 at Lake Quinault Lodge

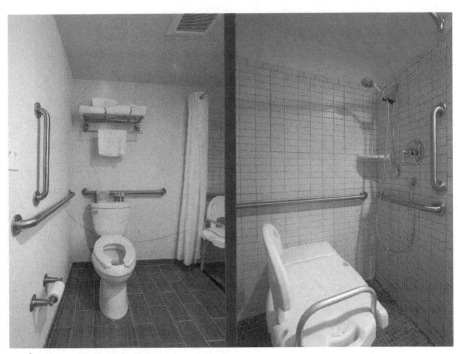
Bathroom in room 402

There is good access to all the public areas of the property, including the indoor pool, the restaurant and the front lobby. The pool is also equipped with a lift.

The lodge is open year-round.

Dining

Roosevelt Dining Room

There is level access to the Roosevelt Dining Room, and plenty of room to maneuver a wheelchair around the tables. Named for the former president who visited the park in 1937, this famous restaurant is open all day. It features a panoramic view of the lake, and a menu sourced with fresh local ingredients. This elegant eatery is a popular dinner choice, so reservations are highly recommended, especially on the weekends.

Olympic National Park Resources

Olympic National Park
(360) 565-3130
www.nps.gov/olym
www.facebook.com/OlympicNPS
twitter.com/OlympicNP

Aramark
(Lake Crescent, Sol Duc and Lake Quinault properties)
(888) 896-3818
www.olympicnationalparks.com

Delaware North
(Kalaloch lodging)
(866) 662-9928
www.thekalalochlodge.com

Mount Rainier National Park

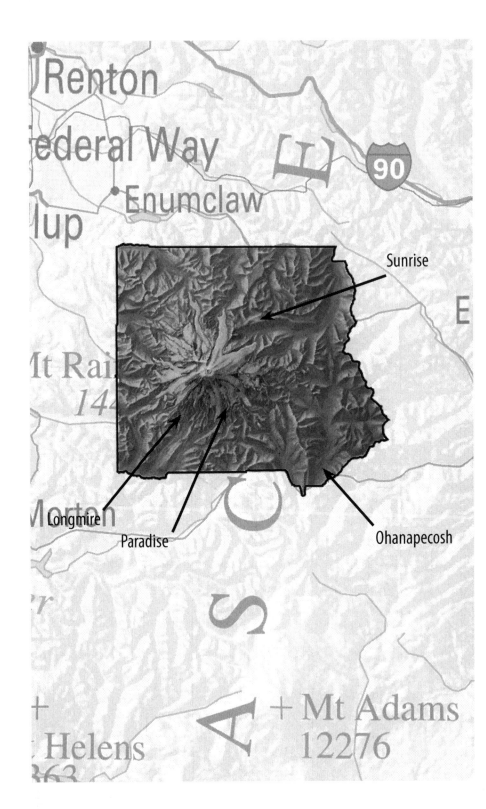

Renton
ederal Way   [H]
up   Enumclaw

                                    Sunrise

Mt Rai   E
14

Longmire
Paradise   Ohanapecosh

Morton

A S C

+ Mt Adams
Helens   12276
63

Located 100 miles southeast of Seattle, Mount Rainier National Park is situated in one of the most rugged areas of Washington State. At 14,410 feet, the namesake mountain towers over the park; and not only is this active volcano the most glaciated peak in the contiguous US, but it's also a popular climb, with over 10,000 attempts each year. That said, you can certainly enjoy the park without attempting the summit, as there are also several developed areas that offer accessible trails, museums, campsites and overnight lodging.

There are four entrances to Mount Rainier National Park.

The Nisqually Entrance is the only vehicle entrance that's open year-round. It's located in the southwest corner of the park, and it provides easy access to Longmire and Paradise. It is also the most popular entrance in the park, as it's just a two-hour drive from the Seattle metro area.

The Stevens Canyon Entrance is located on the southeast corner of the park. It can be accessed from Highway 12 — also known as the White Pass Scenic Byway — and it offers an eastern gateway to Paradise and Longmire.

The White River Entrance, which is the gateway to Sunrise, is located in the northeast corner of the park, off Highway 410.

The Carbon River Entrance, which is located in the northwest corner of the park, is technically open all year; however it's is only open to pedestrian and bicycle traffic.

Mount Rainier from the Trail of the Shadows

And with scenery that ranges from old growth forests and wildflower-filled meadows, to serene mountain lakes and majestic Mount Rainier, there's no shortage of breathtaking views no matter which direction you look in this stunning national park.

The Basics

Road Conditions and Operating Seasons

Although the park is open all year, many of the entrances close seasonally due to harsh weather. The Nisqually Entrance is open year-round, but it's a good idea to call park headquarters and check the current road conditions during the winter months. The Stevens Canyon Entrance is open from late May to early November; while the White River Entrance generally opens on July 1 and closes sometime in late September. The Carbon River Entrance is also open in the winter, but only to pedestrians and cyclists.

The road from Longmire to Paradise usually closes in the evenings beginning in November, but it may reopen in the morning depending on weather conditions. The road to Sunrise closes every night, beginning in late September, and opens the following morning if weather conditions permit. The whole road closes after the first heavy snowfall, which can be as early as October 1.

Conditions can change quickly during the winter months, so it's best to check with park headquarters before you travel. Additionally, vehicles are required to carry tire chains from November 1 to May 1. This applies to all vehicles — even four-wheel drive vehicles and trucks with snow tires — regardless of the weather conditions. For up-to-the-minute updates on road conditions in the park, follow the Mount Rainier National Park twitter feed.

Altitude

Even though namesake Mount Rainier rises up an impressive 14,411 feet above sea level, the majority of the well touristed areas of the park have elevations than range from 1,900 feet to just over 6,000 feet. The highest point in the park reachable by vehicle is Sunrise, which has an elevation of 6,400 feet.

Although the symptoms of altitude sickness generally do not appear at elevations under 8,000 feet, wheelchair-users, slow walkers and people with compromised immune systems may feel the effects of increased altitudes at significantly lower elevations. Symptoms can include headaches, dizziness, shortness of breath, lethargy, insomnia and gastrointestinal disturbances. If you are unfamiliar with the effects that higher elevations have on your body, it's best to take it slow and drink plenty of water for the first few days at any increased elevation, especially if you live at sea level. Additionally, you may want to consult your doctor regarding the effects that increased elevations may have on your specific condition. To assist you in your travel planning, the elevations of all the major areas of the park are listed at the beginning of each section.

Airport

The closest commercial airport to Mount Rainier National Park is Seattle-Tacoma International Airport. It's located approximately two hours northwest of Longmire. Accessible van rentals are available from Wheelchair Getaways (800-642-2042), AMS Mobility (800-854-4176) and Mobility Works (877-275-4915) in the Seattle area. Since there is no park shuttle system, a vehicle is necessary to tour the park.

Connectivity

Cell phone reception is slim to non-existent throughout the park, but there are a couple of pay phones at Jackson Visitor Center for emergencies. Verizon is actively pursuing a project to install an antennae at the visitor center; however that project has not yet been approved by the National Park Service. Either way, the Jackson Visitor Center is the place to connect with the outside world, if need be.

Ranger Programs

Free ranger-led programs are presented during the summer months, and although some include hikes on inaccessible trails, many feature ranger talks at accessible locations. Evening programs are held at the Cougar Rock Campground Amphitheater and the Ohanapecosh Campground Amphitheater, both of which are wheelchair-accessible. Additionally, day and evening ranger talks are held in the lobby of the Paradise Inn, which is also wheelchair-accessible. Consult the park newspaper for the current program offerings.

Wheelchairs

Manual wheelchairs are available for loan at the Sunrise Visitor Center and the Jackson Visitor Center in Paradise. These wheelchairs are only for inside use, and they may not be taken outside of the area.

Camping

Reservations for campsites in the Cougar Rock Campground (in the summer) and the Ohanapecosh Campground can be made online at www.recreation. gov or by phone at (877) 444-6777. Reservations must be made at least four days prior to arrival, and they can be made up to six months in advance.

An America the Beautiful Access Pass is required to occupy an accessible campsite. If nobody has a need for an accessible site, able-bodied campers may be asked to move to a non-accessible site if a qualified person with a disability has a need for the accessible site. Accessible sites may not be reserved by able-bodied campers unless they are the only sites left at the time of reservation.

The Trail of the Shadows

Longmire

Elevation 2,761 Feet

N amed for the man who settled the land, Longmire played an important role in the history of Mount Rainier National Park. Not only is it the site of the first tourist lodging on the mountain, but the original park headquarters was also located there. Today visitors can learn about the past in the museum, take a walk through the woods, or enjoy the Mount Rainier view from the back porch of the historic lodge. And since it's just six miles from the Nisqually entrance, it's also a popular stop for park visitors.

Attractions

Longmire Museum

The Longmire Museum is located across the parking lot from the National Park Inn. There is level access to the building, and although there is room for a wheelchair inside, it can be tight if it gets crowded. The exhibits focus on the geology, natural history and the first settlements in the area. There's also a ranger on duty, and an information desk stocked with plenty of park maps and brochures. And for a blast from the past, don't miss the vintage 1937 tour bus outside, which once transported visitors throughout the park.

Trails

Trail of the Shadows

Located directly across the street from the National Park Inn, the Trail of the Shadows leads through the forest, past beaver lodges and around the site of Longmire's hotel. The hard-packed dirt trail is wide and level and covered with crushed granite. Interpretive plaques about the eruption of Mount Rainier — some 375,000 years ago — line the trail; and there are benches to sit and rest along the way. The east side of the .7-mile loop is accessible, until you reach the old Longmire cabin. After that there are a few steps down to the bridge, and once you cross the creek the trail transitions to an uphill and fairly bumpy path. Still, the first part is a nice stroll through the forest, and quite doable for most wheelchair-users and slow walkers.

Kautz Creek Trail

The Kautz Creek Trail is located across the street from the Kautz Creek Picnic Area. An accessible crosswalk leads across the well traveled park road to the trailhead. A level boardwalk trail winds through the forest that is still recovering from the 1947 glacier generated debris flow, which unleashed a churning mass of mud, rock and vegetation over the area. The boardwalk leads out to an overlook and ends in a crushed granite covered viewing area that has a few benches. There are interpretive plaques about the debris flow along the way, and there's an excellent view of Mount Rainier from the overlook. This new trail is the most accessible offering in the park, so don't miss it.

Picnic Areas

Kautz Creek Picnic Area

The Kautz Creek Picnic Area is located a mile west of Longmire, or about five miles east of the Nisqually entrance. There's accessible parking in front of the accessible vault toilets. Accessible picnic tables are located in a level spot near the parking area. This is one of the most accessible picnic areas in the park, and it's a good choice for a rest stop.

Lodging

National Park Inn

47009 Paradise Road East
Ashford, WA 98304
(855) 755-2275
www.mtrainierguestservices.com

Built in 1906, The National Park Inn proved stiff competition for the Longmire Medical Springs property; and although they enjoyed a healthy rivalry for twenty years, both properties were destroyed in a 1926 fire. Fortunately the inn annex survived the inferno, and today this historic building houses the 25-room National Park Inn.

There's accessible parking near the entrance, with level access to the front lobby. Room 2, which is the most accessible room at the inn, is located just around the corner.

The National Park Inn at Longmire

Room 2 at the National Park Inn

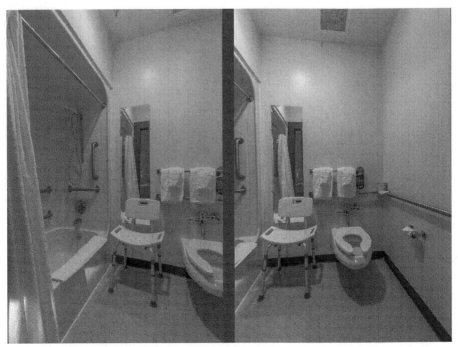

Bathroom in Room 2 at the National Park Inn

The room features wide doorways and it's furnished with a 26-inch high queen-sized with wheelchair access on one side. There is a wide pocket door into the bathroom which is equipped with a tub/shower combination with a hand-held showerhead and a portable shower bench. The toilet grab bars are located on the back and left walls (as seated), and there is a roll-under sink right outside the bathroom.

There is barrier-free access to the public areas of the inn, including the lobby, restaurant and study. There is also level access to the spacious back porch, where you can enjoy an adult beverage and take in the Mount Rainier view.

The National Park Lodge is open year-round.

Cougar Rock Campground

Cougar Rock Campground is located just east of Longmire, on the way to Paradise. Accessible campsites with accessible picnic tables, fire rings and level tent sites are available in Loop C (sites 2, 7 and 20). Accessible restrooms are located nearby. There are also some level usable sites in Loop A and Loop D, depending on your mobility. There is ramp access to the amphitheater, which is located near Loop C, and accessible parking nearby. Campsite C2 is the closest accessible campsite to the amphitheater. Reservations for Cougar Rock Campground are available during the summer months at www.recreation.gov or (877) 444-6777; but during the rest of the year campsites are available on a walk-in basis. This campground is usually open from May to December, but the operating season is highly weather dependent, so check with park headquarters before you make your plans.

Dining

There is level access to the National Park Inn Dining Room, which is located just off the hotel lobby. This casual dining restaurant is open for breakfast, lunch and dinner; and the menu offers a selection old standards, as well as a smattering of Pacific Northwest specialties. There's plenty of room to navigate a wheelchair around the spacious dining room, and the staff is particularly helpful. Like the hotel, the restaurant is open all year.

Services

General Store

The General Store is located next door to the National Park Inn, in a vintage 1911 cabin. There is level access through the front door, with room to navigate a wheelchair around the merchandise. It's stocked with souvenirs, clothing, gifts and works by local artisans.

Paradise Elevation 5,400 Feet

Located 12 miles east of Longmire, this area of the park was named by James Longmire's daughter-in-law, Martha. When she first saw the site she exclaimed, "Oh, what a paradise!" and since it seemed a fitting description, the name stuck. Today Paradise is the site of the main park visitor center, but the big draw here is the summer wildflower display in the adjacent meadows.

Attractions

Jackson Visitor Center

If the architecture of the Jackson Visitor Center seems a bit out of place in contrast to the Paradise Inn, it's because the visitor center was originally designed for a Hawaii site. During the $2.2 million construction project, the structure was reallocated to Mount Rainier, and today this decidedly modern building sits across the parking lot from the historic Paradise Inn. There is accessible parking near the entrance with level access to the building. Inside there's good pathway access to the interpretive exhibits, information desk, food services and accessible restrooms. The visitor

Jackson Visitor Center

center also offers a 360-degree view of Mount Rainier and the surrounding peaks, as well as the showy wildflower meadows.

Trails

Skyline Trail to Lower Myrtle Falls

The trailhead for the Skyline Trail is located on the north side of the upper parking lot, next to the visitor center. This trail is rated as "accessible with assistance", and although it's paved, most wheelchair-users will need some assistance up the initial steep grade. There's only a 100-foot elevation gain on this half-mile trail, but it's all in the same section. If you can get past the steep part, it's pretty level after that. This is the most accessible trail in the Paradise area, and it offers a wonderful view of the wildflowers.

Nisqually Vista Trail

A well-meaning ranger directed me to this trail, saying that it was "mostly accessible". The good news is that there is accessible parking near the trailhead in the lower parking lot. The bad news is that there are 24 steps up to the trailhead. Apparently the ranger figured that since the trail was

Beginning of the Skyline Trail

recommended for strollers, it would be just fine for wheelchairs. It is not, and the only reason I'm including it in this guide is to make people aware of this fact. If you do happen to make it up the 24 steps, you'll encounter a sustained steep grade along the length of the trail. Although there is only a 200-foot elevation gain along the 1.2-mile paved trail, it's a constant up and down, which would be difficult for most wheelchair-users and slow walkers. Have a look at the wildflowers from the visitor center or give the Skyline Trail a try, but don't bother with the Nisqually Vista Trail.

Lodging

Paradise Inn

52807 Paradise Road East
Mount Rainier National Park, WA 98368
(855) 755-2275
www.mtrainierguestservices.com

Built in 1916, the Paradise Inn is one of the few surviving grand old national park lodges. After falling into disrepair the property was slated for demolition, but a vocal protest from an adoring public saved it from the

Paradise Inn

Room 331 at Paradise Inn

wrecking ball. Finally in 1979, the National Park Service spent $1.75 million to replace the failing foundation and repair the existing walls. Today this 212-room inn once again welcomes guests from around the world.

Accessible parking is available in front of the inn, will level access to the front lobby. Room 331, which is located on the lobby level, features wide doorways and good pathway access. It's furnished with two 27-inch high double beds with an access aisle between them, a desk and a chair, a chest of drawers and a nightstand.

The bathroom is equipped with a roll-in shower with grab bars, a hand-held showerhead and a portable shower chair. Although the five-foot turning radius extends into the shower, there's still plenty of room to maneuver a wheelchair. The toilet grab bars are on the left and back walls (as seated), and the roll-under sink is located in the bedroom, in order to free-up more floor space in the bathroom.

There is good wheelchair access to all the public areas of the inn, including the lobby, gift shop and restaurants. An accessible family restroom is located just off the lobby, and the men's and women's restrooms both have accessible stalls.

The Paradise Inn is open from mid-May to October.

Bathroom in room 331 at Paradise Inn

Dining

Paradise Inn Dining Room

The Paradise Inn Dining Room is located just off the lobby, and although there are stairs down to the restaurant, there is a wheelchair lift on the left side. The restaurant is open for breakfast, lunch and dinner, and it offers a nice selection of signature dishes as well as some classic American favorites.

Taboosh Cafe

There is level access to the Taboosh Cafe, which is located off the lobby at the Paradise Inn. There's plenty of room to navigate a wheelchair inside the cafe, which offers a selection of soups, salads, sandwiches and light fare.

Paradise Camp Deli

There's barrier-free access to the Paradise Camp Deli, which is located in the Jackson Visitor Center. Open for lunch, it's a good place to stop for a quick snack, or to grab a sandwich to eat on the trail. The menu includes pizza, soup and salad selections, plus sandwiches, hot entrees, desserts and even ice cream.

Ohanapecosh

L ocated in the southeast corner of the park on Highway 123, Ohanapecosh is 42 miles from the Nisqually entrance and 23 miles from Paradise. This old growth forest is filled with Douglas firs, western red cedars and western hemlocks; and as an added bonus it's usually dry and sunny when Paradise and Longmire are wet and foggy.

Attractions

Ohanapecosh Visitor Center

There's accessible parking in front of the small visitor center, with level access up to the building. Inside there's a book store, some interpretive exhibits and an information desk.

Lodging

Ohanapecosh Campground

Located on the banks of the Ohanapecosh River, this campground has two accessible sites (20 and 21) and an accessible restroom in Loop D. There is also wheelchair access to the amphitheater. Reservations can be made at www.recreation.gov or (877) 444-6777. The campground is open from late May to early October.

Longmire to Sunrise Drive

Elevation 2,761 Feet to 6,400 Feet

One of the most accessible things to do in Mount Rainier National Park is to take the 56-mile scenic drive from Longmire to Sunrise. Although the drive takes about two-and-a-half hours straight through, it's best to allow a whole day for it, as you'll want to stop and enjoy the views along the way, as well as spend some time on top. And although the windshield views are breathtaking on the drive up, they are even more spectacular on the trip back down the hill.

Attractions

Christine Falls

Located just past Longmire, Christine Falls is easy to miss. It's located on the left side of the road, but if you take time to admire it from the road, you'll completely miss the parking area on the right side. The best view of the falls is from the first pullout, which is located directly across the street from the waterfall, before you reach the main parking area. Unfortunately

Christine Falls

there are only stairs down to the lower viewing area, but you can still get a nice view of the top part of the 40-foot high waterfall from the 1928 masonry bridge near the pullout.

Ricksecker Point Loop Drive

The turnoff to Ricksecker Point Road is located about six miles from Christine Falls. This short detour offers good windshield views of Mount Rainier, Nisqually Glacier, Eagle Peak and Rampart Ridge before it rejoins the main road.

Narada Falls

Narada Falls is located eight miles from Ricksecker Point Road. There's a large paved parking lot near the falls, but there are no accessible parking spaces. Although the .2-mile trail to the base of the falls is steep and has steps along the way, you can get a pretty good view of the upper part of the 168-high foot waterfall from the parking lot. There's also an accessible picnic table in the parking lot; however the nearby restrooms are not accessible.

Reflection Lakes

After the road passes Paradise, you'll see Reflection Lakes on your left. The best parking is on the north side of the road, so you might want to catch this stop on the return trip. There is an accessible parking spot on the north side with curb-cut access out to the viewpoint. Even if you don't get out of your car, you'll still get a good view of Mount Rainier's stunning reflection in the lakes.

Sunrise Point

After you exit the Stevens Creek entrance, turn left on Highway 123 to continue on to Sunrise. Follow the road north until you see the turnoff for Sunrise and the White River entrance on your left. From there you'll wind through a series of switchbacks before you reach the ridge top. Sunrise Point is located at the last switchback and it offers a stunning view of the Sourdough Mountains and Sunrise Lake. You don't even have to get out of your car, as you can get a great windshield view from the parking lot.

Sunrise Visitor Center

There is accessible parking near the Sunrise Visitor Center, which is located near the accessible flush toilets. The front entrance to the visitor center has steps, and the ramp from the parking lot is narrow and steep, so it's best to drive behind the restrooms and park near the side entrance, across from the picnic area. There's level access from the side entrance and plenty of room to navigate a wheelchair around the interpretive exhibits. You can get a great view of Mount Rainier from the scope that's trained on the mountain. There is also an accessible picnic table on the other side of the building.

Picnic Areas

Sunrise Picnic Area

The Sunrise Picnic Area is located across the road from the visitor center. There is a paved road leading to the area from behind the restroom, but it may be too steep for some people. That said, people with access issues are allowed to drive on the road to get to the picnic area and the visitor center. There are hard-packed dirt trails to the picnic tables, and there is one site near the road that may work for some slow walkers; but the most accessible picnic tables are located on the visitor center patio.

Dining

Sunrise Snack Bar

The Sunrise Snack Bar is located at the opposite end of the parking lot from the visitor center. There is ramp access up to the entrance, and although the cement ramp is a bit bumpy it's doable for most folks. There's a one-inch lip at the door, and there is plenty of room to navigate a wheelchair inside. The snack bar offers a selection of sandwiches, soups, burgers and soft serve ice cream. Accessible vault toilets are located next door.

Mount Rainier National Park Resources

Mount Rainier National Park

(360) 569-2211

www.nps.gov/mora

www.facebook.com/MountRainierNPS

twitter.com/MountRainierNPS

Rainier Guest Services

(park lodging)

(855) 755-2275

www.mtrainierguestservices.com

North Cascades National Park

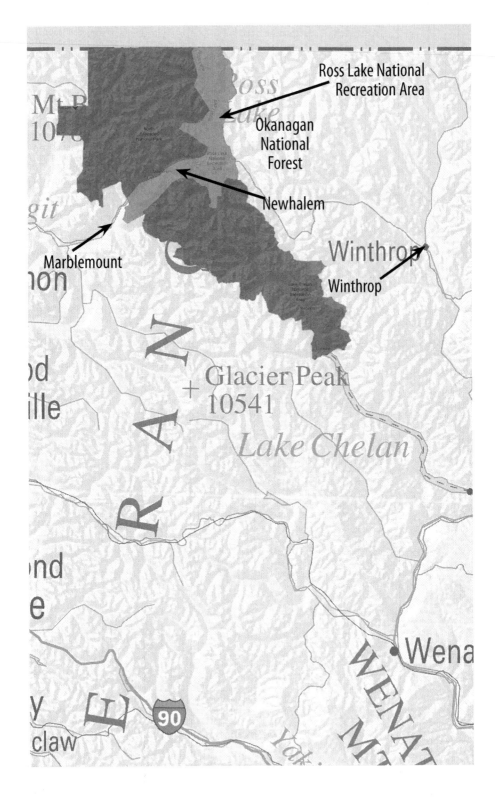

Ross Lake National
Recreation Area

Okanagan
National
Forest

Newhalem

Mt·R
10·

oss
ake

agit

Marblemount

non

Winthrop

Winthrop

od
ille

Glacier Peak
10541

Lake Chelan

nd
e

Wena

y
claw

90

WENAT

RANGE

E

Yak

Nicknamed the "American Alps", North Cascades National Park is one of the most rugged and remote national parks in the US. Filled with black bear, mountain goats and bald eagles, the park is also home to a historic hydroelectric dam. That said you just can't beat the scenery in this northwestern gem, which ranges from jagged mountain peaks, evergreen forests and alpine meadows, to crystal-clear lakes and a collection of formidable glaciers.

The majority of the 500,000-acre natural area is rugged back country, and parts of it are only reachable by gravel roads, four-wheel drive vehicles and an inaccessible shuttle. On the other hand, State Route 20, which bisects the park and borders on a portion of the Ross Lake National Recreation Area, provides access to a nice collection of barrier-free trails, attractions and scenic drives. Additionally, there are some equally scenic diversions, as well as accessible lodging and services, in the land that borders the park on the east and west sides. And even though the Lake Chelan and Stehekin areas of the park don't offer much for wheelchair-users and slow walkers, North Cascades National Park is still well worth a visit for the spectacular scenery and accessible attractions along the accessible State Route 20 corridor.

The Basics

Road Conditions and Operating Seasons

Although North Cascades National Park is open year-round, State Route 20 — also known as the North Cascades Highway — closes in the winter due to heavy snow and avalanches. The road closes between milepost 134 and milepost 178 in late November to mid-December, and reopens in early May. It should be noted that even though the road is open in early spring, the roads to some overlooks and trails near the east side of the park and in the Okanogan National Forest are still covered with snow. The North Cascades Highway Hotline (360-707-5055) provides updated information about the road status. Information about seasonal road closures is also posted on the North Cascades National Park website.

Heavy snow and rain are common during the winter, but summer showers are also possible. The best time to visit the park is from mid-

June to late September, when the roads are cleared and snow isn't in the forecast. Fall is also a pleasant time to visit, as the park is less crowded and the fall colors make for a scenic road trip. It should be noted that weather conditions are quite changeable in this mountain area, so be sure to keep apprised of the forecast during your visit.

Altitude

The highest point in North Cascades National Park is Goode Mountain, which has an elevation of 9,000 feet. That said, the majority of the areas along the North Cascades Highway have an elevation of about 1,500 feet. Rainy Pass (4,855 feet) and Washington Pass (5,477 feet), which are located east of the park in the Okanogan National Forest, are the highest points along the highway.

Although the symptoms of altitude sickness generally do not appear at elevations under 8,000 feet, wheelchair-users, slow walkers and people with compromised immune systems may feel the effects of increased altitudes at significantly lower elevations. Symptoms can include headaches, dizziness, shortness of breath, lethargy, insomnia and gastrointestinal disturbances. If you are unfamiliar with the effects that higher elevations have on your body, it's best to take it slow and drink plenty of water for the first few days at any increased elevation, especially if you live at sea level. Additionally, you may want to consult your doctor regarding the effects that increased elevations may have on your specific condition. To assist you in your travel planning, the elevations of all the major areas of the park are listed at the beginning of each section.

Airport

The closest commercial airport to North Cascades National Park is Seattle-Tacoma International Airport. It's approximately a 2.5-hour drive from the airport to Newhalem. Accessible van rentals are available from Wheelchair Getaways (800-642-2042), AMS Mobility (800-854-4176) and Mobility Works (877-275-4915) in the Seattle area. Since there is no park shuttle service along State Route 20, a private vehicle is necessary to tour the park.

Connectivity

Cell phone reception is marginal to non-existent throughout most of the park. The best place to get a signal is near the North Cascades Visitor Center in Newhalem. Pay phones are also available at the North Cascades Visitor Center and the Skagit Information Center.

Wheelchair Loans

A manual wheelchair is available for loan on a first-come basis at the North Cascades Visitor Center in Newhalem.

Ranger Programs

Ranger-led programs are presented in the Newhalem Creek Campground Amphitheater and at the Diablo Lake Overlook, from the spring through the fall. Access details about these venues are detailed in the lodging and trails listings of this book. For more information about these or additional ranger-led programs, inquire at the North Cascades Visitor Center or call (360) 854-7200.

Camping

Reservations for accessible campsites at Newhalem Creek Campground and the south loop of Colonial Creek Campground can be made at www.recreation.gov or (877) 444-6777. Sites in the north loop of Colonial Creek Campground are available on a first-come basis.

Reservations for accessible sites may require proof of disability upon arrival. If nobody in the party has a need for an accessible site, able-bodied campers may be asked to move to a non-accessible site if a qualified person with a disability has a need for the accessible site. Accessible sites may not be reserved by able-bodied campers unless they are the only sites left at the time of reservation.

Ross Lake National Recreation Area

Elevation 1,604 Feet

L ocated along State Route 20, the Ross Lake National Recreation Area includes three reservoirs, a gaggle of accessible trails, several waterfalls and no shortage of scenic windshield views. Ringed by the mountains these three reservoirs — Ross Lake, Diablo Lake and George Lake — are part of the Skagit Hydroelectric Project, and also provide water gateways to the more remote areas of the national park. And although the Ross Lake National Recreation Area extends up to the Canadian border, the most accessible slice lies in the southern area, in a narrow strip of land adjacent to State Route 20.

Attractions

North Cascades National Park Visitor Center

The North Cascades National Park Visitor Center is located in Newhalem, near the west end of the park, just off State Route 20. Accessible parking is available in front, with level access to the entrance. Inside, there's good wheelchair access around the ranger desk and the interpretive

Ross Lake

exhibits, and over to the accessible restrooms. An introductory film is shown throughout the day in the theater, which features level access and wheelchair seating along the sides. There's also level access to the back patio, where there's an accessible picnic table. A loaner wheelchair is available at the front desk.

Skagit Visitor Information Center

Located just up the road from the North Cascades National Park Visitor Center near milepost 120, the Skagit Visitor Information Center features accessible parking in front, and barrier-free access over to the building. Inside there's good access around the exhibits on the Skagit Project Dams and hydroelectric power, as well as information about Newhalem and the national park. Accessible restrooms are located in front of the building, and there are several standard picnic tables on a level grassy area on the other side of the building. Although the tables aren't technically accessible, there's room enough at the ends for most wheelchairs.

Gorge Creek Falls Overlook

This unusual overlook presents a different vantage point of Gorge Creek Falls. It's located along State Route 20, halfway between Newhalem and the Colonial Creek Campground. There's accessible parking near the road, and accessible restrooms on the far side of the parking lot. The big attractions at this overlook are the two grated footbridges that are located on each side of the highway. There's level access out to the bridges, where you can look down through the grates and get a bird's eye view of Gorge Creek Falls. It's definitely a don't-miss stop.

Diablo Lake Overlook

Located between Colonial Creek Campground and the Ross Lake Overlooks along State Route 20, Diablo Lake Overlook has accessible parking with curb-cut access up to the viewpoints that overlook this deep blue lake. Accessible restrooms are located on the other side of the parking lot, and there's also some accessible picnic tables under the trees. A .3-mile accessible loop trail leads around the lake viewpoints, with interpretive plaques and benches along the way. Not only does this overlook make a nice picnic stop, but it also offers a truly stunning view of the 910-acre lake and the surrounding mountains.

Ross Lake Overlooks

A series of overlooks located along State Route 20 between mileposts 135 and 136 offer some good views of Ross Lake. There's no striped parking in these wide paved pullouts, but you can still get a good windshield view of the lake and the surrounding landscape. They are at least worth a quick stop, even if you don't get out of your vehicle.

Trails

Sterling Munro Boardwalk

This .05-mile boardwalk trail begins to the left of the back patio at the North Cascades National Park Visitor Center. The level trail winds through the forest and out to a viewpoint which offers a nice view of the Picket Range. On a clear day Pinnacle Peak, Crescent Creek Spikes, the Rake, Mt. Terror, Mt. Degenhardt, The Pyramid, Inspiration Peak and the East Towers are visible from the viewpoint. There are also benches and an interpretive plaque at the viewpoint. This easy trail is doable by almost anyone, especially if you make use of the loaner wheelchair that is available at the visitor center.

River Loop

The 1.8-mile section of the River Loop Trail begins to the right of the back patio at the North Cascades National Park Visitor Center. This hard-packed dirt trail travels through the forest, along the Skagit River and past the Newhalem Creek Campground, before it loops back to its origin. And although this trail is rated as accessible, the first part heads downhill and has a number of ruts and obstacles, and would be rough going for most wheelchair-users and slow walkers. The rest of the trail is fairly level, so if you want to dodge the steep section you can pick up the trail between campsites 37 and 38 in Loop B of the Newhalem Creek Campground. From there the tails loops 1.4 miles through the forest, along the river and through the walk-in campground. Accessible restrooms are located in Loop B of the campground; and there's also a hard-packed dirt path to the Loop A accessible restroom, next to walk-in campsite 130 along the trail. Don't let the steep section of this trail deter you from enjoying this pleasant walk through the woods — take the alternate "more accessible" route.

The River Loop Trail

To Know a Tree Nature Trail

The best way to access this trail is to park in the accessible parking space across from the ranger station near the Newhalem Creek Campground. From there follow the hard-packed dirt path towards Loop A and take the first right to connect to the To Know a Tree Nature Trail. This level .5-mile hard-packed dirt trail is topped in stabilized granite and features interpretive plaques along the way. At the trail's end it connects to a portion of the River Loop Trail that travels along the Skagit River, and through the walk-in campground before it circles back to the To Know a Tree Nature Trail. This trail can be done as a short jaunt or a longer hike, depending on your stamina.

Linking Trail

This hard-packed dirt trail links several key sites near the Newhalem Creek Campground and offers an accessible stroll along a fern-lined forest path. It begins across from the ranger station near Loop A of the Newhalem Creek Campground and travels .1 mile to the Newhalem Creek Picnic Area. From there it's another .3 miles to the Rock Shelter Trail, and an additional .25-mile jaunt to the Newhalem Powerhouse.

Rock Shelter Trail

The best way to find the trailhead to the Rock Shelter Trail is to follow the hard-packed dirt Linking Trail from the Newhalem Creek Picnic Area, then turn left when you reach the service road. From there, it's just a short jog across the bridge to the trailhead, which is located on the right. Additionally, the level service road next to Loop C of the Newhalem Creek Campground may provide alternative access to the trailhead, if the road is open. This .3-mile level trail leads over to an old hunting camp sheltered by a large boulder alongside the creek (the rock shelter). This shelter is believed to have been used by Native Americans some 1,400 years ago. This hard-packed dirt trail is level and doable for most wheelchair-users and slow walkers.

Trail of the Cedars

The Trail of the Cedars begins near the suspension bridge, just down the road from the Skagit Visitor Information Center in Newhalem. It's located off of State Route 20, near milepost 120. Accessible parking is available near the visitor center, and on Main Street on the side of Currier Hall, closer to the bridge. A standard picnic table is located on a level cement pad under a tree near the bridge, and although it's not technically accessible, there's room for a wheelchair on the ends.

The .3-mile loop trail, which is maintained by Seattle City Light, starts on the far side of the suspension bridge. Although there is level access on the proximal side of the bridge, some folks will need a little assistance with the two-inch lip on the far side. From there a hard-packed dirt trail covered in stabilized granite winds through the cedar forest, over to the powerhouse and back to the bridge. Part of this area was burned in a fire in 1922, while another section was involved in a 2015 blaze. The remainder of the forest is composed of old growth cedar and some downed nurse logs, and the whole area serves to illustrate the regenerative process of the forest. Interpretive plaques are located along the trail, and although there is one slight uphill portion, the bulk of the trail is fairly level and doable without assistance. You can also access this trail from the end of the Linking Trail. It's a pleasant trail with lots of shade, and it's a great place to beat the heat on a sunny afternoon.

The Gorge Overlook Trail

Gorge Overlook Trail

This scenic trail begins near the accessible restrooms on the far side of the Gorge Creek Falls Overlook parking area. There's ramp access up to a .25-mile paved trail that hugs the shore of Gorge Lake, with interpretive plaques and benches along the way. The trail offers a good view of the Gorge Dam and a distant glance at Gorge Creek Falls. After the last viewpoint the trail transitions to hard-packed dirt and has a 14% downhill grade. It then travels through some rough and rocky areas for another .3-mile, before it loops back to the other side of the Gorge Creek Falls Overlook parking lot. Although the latter section of the trail is not wheelchair-accessible, the paved section makes a nice half-mile out-and-back walk.

Happy Creek Forest Walk

Although the turnoff for this trail lacks adequate signage, it's definitely worth a stop. Start looking for it on the right as you head east on State Route 20, just past milepost 134; and don't feel bad if you have to make a U-turn up the road and double back. Accessible parking is located next to the accessible vault toilet near the trailhead. There's level access over to the .3-mile hard-packed dirt and boardwalk trail through the fir, cedar and hemlock forest. The trail meanders along the creek, as the boardwalk crosses over the cascading waters. This shaded walk through an old growth forest is a cool place to escape the midday heat when the mercury starts to rise.

Picnic Areas

Goodell Creek Raft Launch Picnic Area

This small picnic area — although not officially designated as such — is located at the Goodell Creek Raft Launch Site, off of State Route 20, just west of Newhalem. Look for the turnoff to the Goodell Creek Campground, then follow the signs to the raft launch area. There's parking on a level paved area, and although it's not striped there's room to park parallel and deploy a ramp. The accessible picnic table sits next to the parking area, under a stand of trees on the river's edge. There are no toilets nearby, but it's a pleasant place for a picnic at noon, as the rafters usually launch earlier in the day. That said, if you hit this area at the wrong time of day it can be quite congested, and definitely not conducive to a quiet picnic.

Newhalem Creek Picnic Area

The Newhalem Creek Picnic Area is located across from Loop C of the Newhalem Creek Campground. It features an accessible picnic site with barrier-free access from the accessible parking space over to the accessible picnic table and grill. It's just a short walk over to the accessible restrooms near the group picnic shelter, or over to Loop A of the Newhalem Creek Campground via the Linking Trail. It's a nice secluded picnic site.

Colonial Creek Picnic Area

This small picnic area is located in the South Loop area of Colonial Creek Campground, across the parking lot from the trail out to the accessible fishing pier. It includes accessible picnic tables with accessible restrooms nearby. Accessible parking is also available. It should be noted that the picnic tables are uphill from the fishing pier area, so you'll need to drive down to that area if you want to drop your line.

Lodging

Newhalem Creek Campground

Newhalem Creek Campground is located near the west entrance to the park, just off State Route 20. Campsite 10, which is located in Loop A, features level parking, an accessible picnic table and grill, and an accessible tent platform. It's about 50 feet from the accessible restroom, which has an accessible stall with grab bars and a roll-under sink.

A paved path next to the restroom leads about 100 feet through the forest to the amphitheater. There's level access to the amphitheater, which has bench seating with room on the pavement for wheelchairs on the sides.

Reservations for this campsite may be made from 3 to 360 days in advance at www.recreation.gov.

Campsite 102, which is located in Loop C, has the same accessible features as site 10. This site is located next to the accessible restroom. This loop has been closed, and then sporadically open on a walk-in basis for the past several years, but it will open for advance reservations at www.recreation.gov starting in 2018.

Neewhalem Creek Campground is open from late spring to fall.

Campsite 10 at the Newhalem Creek Campground

Colonial Creek Campground

Located along the shore of Diablo Lake, Colonial Creek Campground is bisected by State Route 20. The majority of the campsites in this campground are located in the South Loop, and are reservable at www.recreation.gov.

Campsite 71 is an accessible walk-in site, and it includes an accessible tent pad, picnic table and grill. It's located close to an accessible parking space on the south side of the highway, and a short roll from the accessible restroom. There's also a .4-mile hard packed dirt trail that leads from the campsite through the forest to an accessible fishing dock on Lake Diablo.

Campsites 113 and 116 are located in the South Loop, near the accessible restroom. They each have accessible parking and include an accessible tent pad, picnic table and grill. There's a paved path from the accessible campsites over to the amphitheater, which offers plenty of room for wheelchair seating in front or on the sides.

Reservations for these three accessible campsites may be made from 3 to 180 days in advance at recreation.gov.

Campsite 30 is located across State Route 20 in the North Loop. It's located near the accessible restroom and it features an accessible tent pad, picnic table and grill. This site is only available on a walk-in basis.

Colonial Creek Campground is open from late spring to fall.

Services

Skagit General Store

Located across from the Skagit Visitor Information Center in Newhalem, the Skagit General Store dates back to 1922, when it was established as an employee commissary for the workers on the Skagit Hydroelectric Project. Today there's accessible parking in front and level access to the store, which is listed on the National Register of Historic Places. It offers a good variety of general grocery items, snacks, sandwiches and camping supplies. The store is also known for its delicious homemade Skagit fudge. It's also the only place along the State Route 20 section of the park that offers anything to eat.

Nearby

Although there aren't very many services inside North Cascades National Park, three nearby areas offer some accessible attractions, restaurants and lodging. And because of the short length of the State Highway 20 corridor, it's easy to spend the day exploring the park, then retreat to the nearby communities for the night.

Marblemount   *Elevation 315 Feet*

Located 15 miles west of Newhalem along State Route 20, the tiny hamlet of Marblemount offers a few restaurants and one hotel that will work for wheelchair-users and slow walkers. It's also a good place to fill up your gas tank before you enter the park.

Lodging

Buffalo Run Inn
60117 State Route 20
Marblemount, WA 98267
(360) 873-2103
www.buffaloruninn.com

This small friendly property has paved parking in front with level access up to the front door. There's no striping in the lot, but it's reserved for hotel guests. There's ramp access up to the front door and plenty of room to maneuver a wheelchair around the common sitting area. That said, guests need to go down to the Buffalo Run Restaurant — which also has level access — to register, as there's no on-site registration desk.

Room 1, which is located right off the common area, has wide doorways and is designated as the wheelchair- accessible room. It's furnished with a table and chair, a refrigerator, an easy chair, two night tables and a 28-inch high queen-sized bed with wheelchair access on the left side (as you face it).

The bathroom is outfitted with a roll-in shower with a hand-held showerhead, grab bars and a fold-down shower bench. There is a two-inch lip on the shower, but because of the placement of the shower bench, it's easy to dodge with a direct transfer. The toilet has grab bars on the back and left walls (as seated) and the bathroom also has a pedestal sink.

All in all it's a very functional room that will work for most wheelchair-users.

There's also level access to the breakfast room, which is adjacent to the common area. A Continental breakfast, including fruit, cereal, pastries and coffee is served daily. Guests of the inn also receive a 10% discount at the Buffalo Run Restaurant, which is open for lunch and dinner.

Room 1 at the Buffalo Run Inn

Dining

Buffalo Run Restaurant
60084 State Route 20
Marblemount, WA 98267
(360) 873-2461
www.buffaloruninn.com

Located on the main drag, there's accessible parking near the door, with level access over to the front entrance of this casual steakhouse. Although there are steps down to the back patio, there's wheelchair access to the inside tables. Open for lunch and dinner, this eatery serves a variety of game meats including everything from elk to kangaroo. The menu includes fresh fish, daily specials and vegetarian options; and they also have a nice selection of organic beers.

Mondo Restaurant
60102 State Route 20
Marblemount, WA 98267
(360) 873-2111
www.facebook.com/Mondos-Restaurant-1584747858460183/

Open for breakfast, lunch and dinner, this restaurant has a level entrance and ample wheelchair seating inside. The menu includes a hearty selection of traditional favorites for breakfast, and a variety of sandwiches and Asian entrees for lunch and dinner. The prices are quite reasonable, and it's the only place in town that's open for breakfast.

Okanogan National Forest *Elevation 1,768 Feet to 5,476 Feet*

L ocated on the east side of North Cascades National Park, the
Okanogan National Forest offers a scenic view of the rugged Cascades
along State Route 20. And if you'd like to stop for a closer look, there are
also a few accessible trails and overlooks along the way.

Attractions

Rainy Lake National Recreation Trail
Located about 10 miles east of North Cascades National Park, Rainy Pass is
home to the very accessible Rainy Lake National Recreation Trail. Located
near milepost 158, there's accessible parking and level access to the trailhead
at the south end of the parking lot. This one-mile paved trail leads out to
a viewpoint on Rainy Lake. Near the half-mile point another inaccessible
trail branches off to the right, but the accessible trail continues along on the
left to the lake. It's a two-mile out-and-back hike, but the view of the lake
surrounded by the towering Cascades is definitely worth the effort.

Washington Pass Overlook
At 5,476 feet, Washington Pass is the highest point along the North
Cascades Highway. Located about four miles east of Rainy Pass, it's a
required stop on any national park itinerary. Accessible parking and
vault toilets are located near a 400-foot paved trail out to the overlook.
From there, steps and a steep grade prevent wheelchair-users and slow
walkers from going any further; however the views of Liberty Bell and
Early Winter Spires from the lower viewpoint are excellent. It's also a
good vantage point for the fall colors. Accessible picnic tables and an
information station are located in the parking area, and this site makes
a good lunch stop. And if you don't want to walk over to the viewpoint,
you can also get a good windshield view from the parking lot. It should be
noted that the service road up to the parking lot is covered in snow and
closed to vehicular traffic until early July. For Information on current trail
conditions contact the Winthrop Ranger Station at (509) 996-4000.

Winthrop   *Elevation 1,768 Feet*

The old west town of Winthrop makes a nice side trip while you're in the area. Make a day out of it, and stop at the scenic viewpoints on State Route 20 in the Okanogan National Forest along the way. Accessible parking is available in the Red Barn Community Center, on the right as you roll into town. From there, it's about a quarter-mile walk to Riverside Avenue, which is lined with boardwalk sidewalks and filled with restaurants and quaint shops. For the most part the sidewalks are wheelchair-accessible and about 60 percent of the businesses have a level entrance. There is also parallel parking available along Riverside Avenue near the Duck Brand Hotel and Cantina, and in front of the real estate office. A number of casual restaurants offer level access and serve up pizza, sandwiches, burgers and ice cream. There's also level access to Confluence Park, which is located across the street from the Duck Brand Hotel and Cantina. Although it's a tiny park, it features level access over to a riverside viewpoint which boasts a few benches to relax and take in the scenery. Winthrop is definitely a tourist town, but it makes a fun lunch stop while you're in the area.

View from the Washington Pass Overlook

North Cascades National Park Resources

North Cascades National Park
(360) 854-7200
www.nps.gov/noca
www.facebook.com/NorthCascadesNationalPark
twitter.com/NCascadesNPS

Access Resources

Emerging Horizons

www.EmergingHorizons.com
Your one-stop accessible travel resource.

- Destinations
- Lodging Options
- Tour Companies
- Travel News
- Trails & Recreation
- Travel Tips

Barrier-Free National Parks

www.barrierfreenationalparks.com
Access information on some of America's top national parks.

- Insider Tips
- Resources
- Suggested Itineraries
- Access Photos

Barrier-Free Travel
Utah National Parks
FOR WHEELERS AND SLOW WALKERS

By Candy B. Harrington

This handy guide includes detailed information about accessible trails, sites, lodging options, tours, transportation and attractions in Zion, Bryce Canyon, Capitol Reef, Arches and Canyonlands National Parks. Along with detailed information about trails and viewpoints that will work for wheelchair-users and slow walkers, it also includes detailed descriptions of all the in-park lodging options, along with photographs of the accessible rooms. Access details and photos of 23 additional accessible lodging options near the parks are also included, as well as information on accessible campsites in the parks.

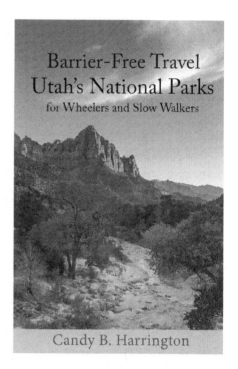

Top it off with information about ranger-led tours, loaner wheelchairs and the free America the Beautiful Access Pass and you have a very comprehensive resource.

www.barrierfreeutah.com

Barrier-Free Travel
Yosemite, Sequoia
AND
Kings Canyon National Parks
FOR WHEELERS AND SLOW WALKERS

By Candy B. Harrington

This indispensable guidebook includes detailed access information that will help wheelchair-users and slow walkers find an accessible room and build a barrier-free itinerary in Central California's top three national parks. Along with updated information about accessible trails, boardwalks, viewpoints, museums and picnic areas, this helpful resource also includes detailed access evaluations and photographs of 33 properties in and near the parks. And if you'd like to sleep under the stars, barrier-free campsites are also noted. Add in helpful details about the location of local airports, and the availability of accessible shuttles, public transportation and van rentals, and you've got all the information you need to get to and around the parks. Top it off with information on accessible bus tours, ranger programs, wheelchair and handcycle rentals and you have a must-have resource for wheelchair-users, stroller parents or anybody who just needs to take things a little slower.

www.barrierfreeyosemite.com

Q&As with Candy Harrington

Why Washington National Parks? What's so special about them?

Well they certainly each offer their own rugged beauty, and they are close enough together to do in one trip; but the driving force behind this book was the glut of misinformation out there regarding access in these parks. Misinformation is worse than no information at all, so I decided it was time to let folks know what exactly was out there access wise. I discovered a lot of trails that were rated as "accessible with assistance" really had varying degrees of access, so I did what I always do — I described the access so folks can decide if they will or won't work for them. After all, "accessible with assistance" is a very ambiguous term.

Isn't this really the second edition of this title?

Not exactly. My previous title only included Olympic and Mount Rainier National Parks, and was titled as such. This book also includes North Cascades; hence the new "Washington National Parks" title.

So why didn't you include North Cascades National Park in your previous title?

Unfortunately I listened to too many nay-sayers who told me that there was nothing for my readers up there. And when I subsequently discovered that just wasn't true, I had to correct the omission. I thought the easiest way to do that was to craft a inclusive book of all of Washington's national parks.

North Cascades National Park is largely backcountry. Are there really accessible things to do there? What about lodging?

Yes, there is a large backcountry area of the park, but I also found a lot of accessible trails along State Highway 20, especially near Newhalem. It's amazing what's out there, as it's not really publicized. Unfortunately there are no hotels in the national park, but I did highlight a nice accessible inn nearby.

Mount Rainer seems pretty rugged too. Is it really a good choice for wheelchair-users?

Mount Rainier is over 14,000 feet high and some 10,000 climbers attempt to summit it every year; but the great thing is, you can also enjoy its beauty from afar. There's a great view of the mountain from the end of the accessible Kautz Creek Trail, and you can also get a good view of it from the Visitor Center at Sunrise — they even have an accessible scope trained on the mountain. So yes, even though it is pretty rugged, there are still lots of offerings for wheelchair-users and slow walkers.

I've heard that access is improving in the near future in Olympic National Park. Is that true?

Absolutely. When the upgrades to the Spruce Railroad Trail are completed in 2019, it will effectively triple the length of accessible trail offerings in Olympic National Park.

Did you encounter any problems while researching these parks for the book?

Unfortunately yes. Because of the misinformation out there I had a lot of false leads, which made my site visits all that more time consuming. I put a lot of time in on my research and I trekked down every possible trail to see if it might be suitable for my readers. It was a lot of work, but on the plus side, the weather was good and I discovered some absolutely beautiful places.

How would you rate the access in these parks compared with that of the Grand Canyon?

Well that's like comparing apples to oranges. The Grand Canyon is one of America's most visited national parks, while the Washington National Parks are more remote. There are more accessible facilities in the Grand Canyon, but on the other hand there are more people competing for them. In Washington I strolled through peaceful rainforests, and lingered at scenic overlooks that were virtually deserted; and that's something I just can't do in the Grand Canyon. On the other hand, there's no Skywalk in Washington. If you just look at the accessible trails, facilities and lodges, the Grand Canyon certainly has more; however if you look at the remoteness and peaceful quality of the those features, then the Washington parks definitely win.

Did you actually look at all the hotels you covered, or did you just interview the managers?

I inspected each and every property that I covered. I never rely on second-hand information in any of my work, and although it takes a bit more effort, I feel it's worth it.

Are there hotels with roll in showers in the parks?

Absolutely — both Olympic and Mount Rainier have accessible rooms with roll-in showers. North Cascades has no lodging in the park, but I did cover a nearby inn with a roll-in shower.

Why did you also include lodges that were outside of the parks?

Because these parks are so remote, I wanted to give my readers more choices. After all, most of the lodging offerings in the parks only have a few accessible rooms. But it's not like I covered lodging options in Seattle — truly the properties that I selected are close to the parks, and very convenient for day visits.

What is your favorite thing to see or do in these parks?

I really love the diversity in all of the parks, but if I have to pick one favorite place it's got to be Lake Crescent. The accessible room at the lodge is near the lakeshore and it's pleasant to sit on the back porch and enjoy the view. There is also a nice accessible trail nearby, that winds through the forest and out along the shore. Plus there is a cool glassed-in porch in the main lodge that's the perfect place to enjoy the sunset with a glass of wine.

What's the next title in your Barrier-Free Travel series?

Next up is *Barrier-Free Travel; Glacier, Yellowstone and Grand Teton National Parks*. It will be released in late spring 2018. www.barrierfreeyellowstone

46367736R00060

Made in the USA
Middletown, DE
27 May 2019